LEGENDS A
OF

BRADWELL
BOOKS

Published by Bradwell Books

9 Orgreave Close Sheffield S13 9NP

Email: books@bradwellbooks.co.uk

British Library Cataloguing in Publication Data: a catalogue record for this book is available from the British Library.

1st Edition

ISBN: 9781909914988

Print: Gomer Press Limited, Llandysul, Ceredigion SA44 4JL

Design by: Andrew Caffrey

Typesetting by: Mark Titterton

Photograph Credits: IStock and the author

Cover Photographs

Background image: Shutterstock/ Panos Karas

Green man image: Shutterstock/ Gwoeii

Castle and flag image: IStock

CONTENTS

Brochwel, Prince of Powys, sets his hounds on the hare protected by St Melangell, in a striking illustration by Willy Pogany (see the 'Heroes and Saints' chapter).

INTRODUCTION

The folklore and legends of Wales are among the oldest and the most exciting. Many survive in ancient manuscripts, such as the 'Red Book of Hergest' and the 'White Book of Rhydderch', both dating from the 14th century but almost certainly referencing much earlier sources. In the middle of the 19th century many of these surviving stories were compiled and translated into English by Lady Charlotte Guest as *The Mabinogion*. Some of the oldest stories featuring King Arthur appear in *The Mabinogion* and are therefore of worldwide importance.

In addition to such epics, there is a wealth of local legends, yarns and strange superstitions recorded from throughout the Principality. These are, in their way, arguably all the more

The fairies visit the market at Laugharne, in Carmarthenshire.

Llyn y Dywarchen in Gwynedd, with the peak of Snowdon above it. In the Middle Ages the lake was recorded as possessing a floating island. It was also renowned as a place resorted to by the fairies and where at least one fairy bride was captured.

interesting to the average reader in that they reveal the very real beliefs of our recent ancestors. Most people living in the Welsh countryside in the 18th and 19th centuries firmly believed in the existence of fairies, ghosts, witchcraft and even – in one or two communities – dragons.

For the purposes of this necessarily brief introduction to the folk tales of Wales, I have focused in on these less well-known stories and accounts. In them you will meet a wide variety of strange beings and fascinating characters, such as the elegant, aristocratic but dangerously amoral Fair Tribe; the crafty old lady who fooled the Devil; wicked witches and helpful healers; the saint who lost her head and got it back again; the woman who had to fend off a fiendish version of her husband in the bedroom; and the man who had to lean against a cow for comfort after being spooked by a scary ghost.

The folklore of Wales paints it as a wonderfully magical place. Many would say this is still true today.

THE FAIR TRIBE

Throughout the British Isles, and further afield, there was for centuries a firm belief in a separate order of beings, human in appearance and customs, who regularly visited our world but were not part of it. Generically, they are known as the fairies.

In Wales the fairies were referred to by a number of names. *Y Tylwyth Têg*, translated as 'the Fair Folk or Tribe', was perhaps the most common. The English employed similar euphemisms, such as 'the Good Neighbours'. It was considered sensible to always keep on the right side of the fairies: you never knew when one might be listening. Another Welsh name for them was the *Bendith y Mamau*, or 'Blessing to Mothers'. Fairies were known to steal human children (see below), and this compliment may have been another attempt to keep them agreeable. The more general Welsh word for 'fairy' was *ellyll* (plural *ellyllon*), similar to the English 'elf'. However, the meaning of the word is closer to that of 'goblin', something weird and grotesque, rather than the elegant, aristocratic *Tylwyth Têg*.

The fairies of Wales took many forms. They might be as tiny as birds, a few feet tall or the same size as humans. Unlike the fairies of Ireland and the rest of the UK, they tended to dress in blue rather than the combination of red and green which tends to be thought of as the traditional fairy colours. In the unique case of the fairies of Pentrefoelas, in Conwy, they dressed uniformly in grey. More often the *Tylwyth Têg* would simply adopt the myriad finery equally enjoyed by the human aristocracy.

Welsh fairies could be malicious or generous. More often they were amoral, their treatment of the humans they encountered depending entirely on the person's behaviour towards them. A few mortals enjoyed excellent relations with them but they were unpredictable and swift to revenge supposed slights or disrespect. What made them more dangerous was their continual campaign to inveigle people into their world, which they achieved by tempting them to join in one of their dances – fairies love dancing – or by promising a life of luxury and ease. This could prove fatal to their victims. Time runs at a different rate in fairyland. The dancing may seem to go on for a few pleasant hours, but in reality weeks, years or even centuries may pass by in the mortal world while it lasts. Fairy revels usually involved a feast after the dancing, but woe betide the mortal man or woman who joined in. By consuming fairy food and drink they became part of the fairy world and were unable to safely return to our world.

In the case of one unlucky Carmarthenshire man, simply sitting and enjoying the song of an enchanted bird was sufficient to bring about his doom. An American resident in Cardiff in the 1870s, Wirt Sikes, took a strong interest in the folk tales of his adopted country and learnt the following story from a farmer's wife who lived near the scene of the action. This was a hollow, infamous as a fairy haunt, called Pant Shon Shenkin after the unlucky hero of the story.

In his book *British Goblins,* Sikes writes: 'As he [Shon Shenkin] was going afield one fine summer's morning, he heard a little bird singing, in a most enchanting strain, on a tree close by his path. Allured by the melody, he sat down under the tree until the music ceased, when he arose and looked about him. What was his surprise at observing that the tree, which was grown and full of life when he sat down, was now withered and barkless! Filled with astonishment, he returned to the farmhouse which he had left, as

A friend succeeds in rescuing a man about to be inveigled into a fairy dance. An illustration by T.H. Thomas from British Goblins*, published in 1880.*

he supposed, a few minutes before; but it also was changed, grown older, and covered with ivy.'

In the farmhouse doorway stood an old man Shon did not recognise. He demanded to know what he did there, and was told in no uncertain terms that he was the owner of the house.

'How is this?' asked Shon. 'Where's my father and mother, whom I left here a few minutes since, whilst I have been listening to the charming music under yon tree, which when I rose was withered and leafless?'

The truth dawns on the old man, if not on Shon, and he asks him his name. On learning it, he replies: 'Alas, poor Shon, and this is indeed you! I often heard my grandfather, your father, speak of you and long did he bewail your absence. Fruitless inquiries were made for you; but old Catti Maddock of Brechfa said you were under the power of the fairies and would not be released until the last sap of that sycamore would be dried up. Embrace me, my dear uncle, for you are my uncle – embrace your nephew.'

But when the two men embrace, poor Shon – who should have been dead and in his grave decades ago – crumbles into dust on the doorstep.

Many believe that fairies are the equivalent of ghosts and that they were originally perceived as spirits of the dead. According to this theory, fairyland was by extension the underworld. In one of our earliest accounts of fairy-like beings from Wales – indeed from the whole of the UK – there seems no question that it is the dead who are being observed. In a tale recorded in the 12th century by the Monmouthshire scribe Walter Map, a nobleman comes across a number of unearthly lords and ladies dancing in a ring near his castle. Among the dancers he recognises his deceased wife.

It's interesting that the Welsh fairyland, called Annwn, could only be reached by descending underground or beneath lakes. Some fairies inhabited ancient burial mounds. Annwn was invariably described as a place of permanent twilight where nothing was really substantial. Fine wine is proved to be rainwater, fine clothes autumn leaves and gold coins cockle shells.

Those the fairies sought to lure to their world were invariably youths or men. It has been suggested they may represent a folk memory of a Bronze Age people, ousted by the more advanced Iron Age Celts, who were seeking to replenish their genetic stock by enticing men from other tribes to join them. This might explain the number of 'fairy bride' stories from Wales. In these stories, young men meet beautiful fairy women and marry them, with certain conditions placed upon the union. The most common of these is that the husband must never allow his fairy wife to come into contact with iron – an intriguing hint here that the fairies may indeed have been Bronze Age people. Inevitably, the woman is accidentally struck

The fairy-enchanted Shon ap Shenkin crumbles to dust in the arms of his nephew, now an old man. Another illustration from British Goblins.

with something made of iron and she immediately returns to her people. By this time, a number of half-human, half-fairy children would have been born. At one time many people liked to claim fairy ancestry in Wales.

When the *Tylwyth Têg* failed to gain fresh human stock by other means, they might resort to forcible abduction. The so-called 'fair tribe' had an unpleasant habit of stealing human children and replacing them with 'changelings'. Changelings were fairies disguised by magic to resemble the stolen infant. The fake baby would enjoy being pampered while giving his or her partners in crime the chance to get away with the real one. Welsh mothers would hang a pair of scissors above the cradle to ward off the fairies. This rather dangerous practice was thought to work because not only were the scissors made of iron or steel (and iron, as we know, is inimical to the fairies), they would also hang in the shape of a cross.

Despite its appearance, the changeling would give itself away by its bad behaviour and a knowing look in its eye. Or it might not thrive and remain a grizzling weakling. In order to ensure their child was returned, the parents might find it necessary to threaten the life of the changeling.

The Revd Elias Owen recounts a story of changeling twins in his exceptional work on *Welsh Folklore* published in 1896. In the story, a farming couple from Trefeglwys in Powys became concerned that their twin infants were lethargic and failing to grow. The wife consulted a *Dyn Hysbys* (a wise man) and he suggested she employ an elaborate ritual to determine the twins' true nature. Harvest was coming up and it was the custom for all the wives to cook up a stew to feed the men who would be reaping the corn. On this occasion, in full view of the infants, the mother began to make the stew inside a single egg-shell. After she had accomplished this bizarre procedure, she went outside, as if satisfied with her work, and secretly listened at the door. She was amazed to hear one of the 'babies' speaking to the other. It said:

'Gwelais fesen cyn gweled derwen,
Gwelais wy cyn gweled iâr,
Erioed ni welias verwi bwyd i fedel
Mewn plisgyn wy iâr!'

Which translates as:

'Acorns before oak I knew,
An egg before a hen,
Never one hen's egg-shell stew
Enough for harvest men!'

Clearly these were no human babies. Now certain her children had indeed been stolen by the fairies, the woman snatched up the two changelings and carried them, yelling and complaining, to a nearby lake, Llyn Ebyr. Taking each by the ankle, she prepared to throw them in, but just then a group of *Tylwyth Têg* appeared and hurriedly handed over her babies in place of the imperilled changelings.

Up until the 18th century, belief in fairies was still strong and it is a sad truth that many children born with certain disabilities might be labelled changelings. Even a reasonably well-educated Christian man like the Revd Edmund Jones, a Nonconformist preacher resident in Blaenau Gwent, could fall into this error. In 1779, he wrote of the son of one Edmund John William, who had been stolen away, 'leaving an idiot in his stead'. With a chilling lack of compassion, Jones continues: 'He lived longer than such children used to live, until he was (I think) ten or twelve years of age. I saw

The Fairy Oak illustrated in Thomas Pennant's** History of Whiteford and Holywell,* ***published in 1796.

him myself: there was something diabolical in his aspect, but more of this in his motion and voice – for his motions were mad and he made very disagreeable screaming sounds which frightened some strangers who passed by. His complexion was a dark, tawny colour.' Was this an autistic child or one with Down's syndrome? The fact that he 'lived longer than such children used to live' hints at the type of treatment similarly unfortunate youngsters might expect. In the same century, the well-known author and traveller Thomas Pennant noted another example of the belief in changelings.

Pennant lived at Downing Hall near Whitford in Flintshire. In the grounds of Downing Hall there was a magnificent oak tree with long spreading branches. It was known as the Fairy Oak. Pennant recalled: 'A poor cottager, who lived near the spot, had a child who grew uncommonly peevish; the parents attributed this to the fairies, and imagined that it was a changeling. They took the child, put it into a cradle, and left it all night beneath the tree, in hopes that the *Tylwyth Têg* ... would restore their own before the morning. When morning came, they found the child perfectly quiet, so went away with it, quite confirmed in their belief.'

It must have been a strong belief indeed to have exposed their child to the rigours of a cold night in the open air.

TWO FAIRY HAUNTS

Surprisingly, one of the earliest sources we have for fairy stories in Wales comes from a book called *Fairy Legends and Traditions of the South of Ireland*. The book, by Thomas Crofton Croker, is in three volumes, of which the third, published in 1828, is largely given over to tales of fairies collected not from the South of Ireland but from South Wales.

The reason for this is that after the publication of his first two volumes, Croker received a mountain of fan mail from a lady resident in Aberpergwm, in the Vale of Neath. Miss Jane Williams had taken upon herself the task of collecting fairy traditions from her own part of the world, having been inspired by Croker's example. She gleaned many interesting tales from her neighbours and from rural labourers. In one of her letters to Croker, Miss Williams admitted that she was surprised to find just how many people believed in fairies in her neighbourhood.

'Many of my old friends are highly respectable in their line of life, farmers and farmers' wives, of strict veracity on all other topics save supernatural agencies; and they relate these stories with an earnestness and an air of truth that is perfectly confounding,' she writes.

Miss Williams continues that 'some have actually seen the fairies', citing as an example 'old Shane of Blaenllanby'. This venerable lady told Miss Williams that one evening she had seen approaching her 'several hundreds' of the Fair Tribe.

'It was almost dusk,' writes Miss Williams, 'and they were not a quarter of a mile from her. They were very diminutive persons, riding four a-breast, and mounted upon small white horses, not bigger than dogs. They formed a long cavalcade, and passing on towards the mountain, at a place called Clwydau'r Banwen, they disappeared behind the high ground, and seemed to be traversing the Sarn, or ancient Roman road, which crosses that mountain.'

Miss Williams would take down the stories directly from the lips of the storyteller. Thomas Croker reproduced many of these stories in his book. To open one of these stories, about a boy being stolen by the fairies, the narrator, a Mr John Jones, a cobbler of nearly 90 years of age, insists: 'I tell you the fairies were to be seen in the days of my youth by the thousand, and I have seen them myself a hundred times.'

He goes on to explain that so anxious was he to see the fairy tribe for himself that he asked a gypsy woman, skilled in mysterious lore, to help him achieve this ambition. She tells him: 'Go and find a clover with four leaves and bring nine grains of wheat, and put them on this leaf in this book.'

The gypsy removed a little book from her pocket and handed it to Jones. She then told him that, having accomplished these tasks, he should meet her by moonlight on the following night, the rendezvous being the summit of Craig y Dinas, a mighty crag that overlooks the Vale of Neath. Mr Jones did all the gypsy woman asked, and she took out a phial and washed his eyes with the contents.

'As soon as I opened my eyes,' he said, 'I saw at a short distance thousands of little people all in white, dancing in a circle to the sound of at least a score of harps. After dancing for some time, they left the circle, and formed a line on the brow of the hill; the one next the precipice squatted down, clasped her hands under her knees and tumbled, tumbled, tumbled, head-over-heels, all the way down the hill; the rest all followed her example, until they were lost in the dark wood of the valley beneath.'

Miss Williams had presumably gathered a number of well-known local storytellers together, for Mr Jones then called on another elderly fellow, Morgan Gwillim, to confirm that he, too, had seen the fairies. Mr Gwillim does so and goes on to list a number of natural features in the neighbourhood of Aberpergwm where he witnessed their antics. Of particular note is a waterfall he names 'Cylepsta'. This is almost certainly the celebrated falls on the Afon Hepste today known as Sgwd yr Eira, the 'fall of snow'. It is possible to walk behind this beautiful waterfall as it creates a curtain of white water dropping over a projecting ledge of sandstone.

'I never saw [the fairies] to such perfection,' states Mr Gwillim, 'as when I stood between the cascade and the rock over which it fell. I could at that moment see them distinctly glittering in all the colours of the rainbow and hear their music softly blending with the murmur of the waterfall. After enjoying themselves here for some time, they all proceeded into a small cave, which they had made in the rock, where they seemed to be exceedingly amused, laughing and having a great deal of merriment. Then they ascended the rock, and frisked away, the sound of their melodious harps dying away among the mountains, whither they had fled.'

These descriptions of the fairies are very Shakespearian: jolly, diminutive little fellows sporting about and presenting no threat to anybody. Croker's use of stories such as these gave the Vale of Neath, and Craig y Dinas in particular, the reputation of being the most fairy-haunted place in Wales. In fact, this is just an indicator of just how rich Wales was in fairy traditions at this time. It seems reasonable to suppose that if anyone living elsewhere in Wales had shared Miss Williams's enthusiasm for collecting such stories, we would have found them surviving to a similar extent.

A mid-19th century engraving of the waterfall on the Afon Hespte where the fairies were said to be seen romping about.

Later on in the century, the folklorist Elias Owen discovered a smaller pocket of fairy belief in the wild expanse of moorland known as the Hiraethog. The word *hiraeth* means something like 'longing' or 'homesickness' and may suggest a mournful, affecting landscape. The area remains sparsely populated today. This isolation, combined with its wild aspect, may be the reason fairy traditions lingered here longer than most places in Wales.

A local farmer, Thomas Jones, was Owen's source. He said that a few years before their conversation in the 1880s, a party of children had seen the fairies on a neighbouring hill. Low cloud had capped the hill and the children saw 'a large number of diminutive folk, dressed in blue' emerging from the mist and then rushing back into it, as if startled at finding themselves observed.

In addition, Mr Jones informed Owen that 'it was well known' thereabouts that the grandmother of one of his neighbours had been great friends with the *Tylwyth Têg*. 'Mrs R' (Owen does not provide her full name) was on such good terms with the fairies that they had a nickname for her, 'Aunty Ann'. On the edge of the Clocaenog Forest, at Bod Petrual, there is a small lake where Aunty Ann would go to gather rushes. Here she would often encounter the Fair Tribe. Their little dogs would run up to greet her, 'just as any other dog would come to welcome its master's friend'.

Another legend of the Hiraethog involves a fairy cow, which had the magical ability to supply unlimited quantities of milk, to the great benefit of the neighbourhood. She was called the *Fuwch Frech* (Speckled Cow) and she had her home among prehistoric earthworks now obscured beneath the conifer trees of Clocaenog Forest. Unfortunately, an evil witch milked and milked the *Fuwch Frech* into a sieve until she ran dry. After this cruel deed was enacted upon her, the cow returned to fairyland.

Bringing us into the new millennium, a resident of the Hiraethog, Judy Young, found in the midst of a remote forest what she could only describe as a 'fairy house'. It was a kind of wigwam, composed of twigs, leaves and pine-needles, and had been intricately constructed with considerable skill. A neat fence of interwoven twigs surrounded it. It was just about big enough for a mouse to live in. Ms Young had walked her dogs in these isolated woods on many previous occasions and rarely saw anyone else in them. Of course, she didn't believe there was anything supernatural about the little 'house', but it remains a mystery as to who visited that lonely place in order to manufacture this unique and tiny artefact and why they should choose to do so. Even stranger, when Ms Young returned to the forest to show the 'fairy house' to some friends, she was amazed to discover that it had vanished. She found the right spot without any trouble, but of the little wigwam there was no sign. I reproduce Judy Young's photo of the 'fairy house' in my book *Wales of the Unexpected* (Gwasg Carreg Gwalch, 2005).

The beautiful little lake at Bod Petrual, where Aunty Ann used to meet the fairies.

LAND OF THE DRAGON

Wales is one of the few nations to feature a mythical creature on its flag: *Y Ddraig Goch*, 'The Red Dragon'. The Red Dragon first appears in a story entitled 'Lludd and Llefelys' in the *Mabinogion*. In this story the Red Dragon is constantly battling with a White Dragon, and their screams of rage and pain disturb the neighbourhood to the extent that crops fail and pregnant women miscarry. On the advice of the King of France, the British king Lludd digs a pit and fills it with mead. The battling beasts fall into the pit and end up consuming the mead, which puts them both into a drowsy stupor.

Lludd has the sleeping dragons carted off to a cavern deep below a mountain in North Wales which later came to be known as Dinas Emrys (the 'City of Emrys'). In time they awaken and once again begin their squabbling, but with far less disturbance for the people of Britain. Centuries later, the rapacious British king Vortigern spots Dinas Emrys as an ideal place to build a fortress. However, the struggles of the dragons down below create earth tremors which cause the walls to fall as soon as they are erected. Unaware of the monsters' existence, Vortigern believes himself to have been cursed and seeks out a great, if remarkably young, wizard named Ambrose (in later sources identified as Merlin), for an end to his problem.

Ambrose reveals the existence of the dragons and they are released from their prison. Vortigern and his court watch in amazement as the Red Dragon, after a fierce final scrap, defeats the WhiteDragon.

Then Ambrose-cum-Merlin explains to Vortigern that the Red Dragon represents the British (i.e. Welsh) people and the White Dragon the outsiders invading from over the seas (the Angles, Saxons, Jutes etc.). As demonstrated by the dragons, the Welsh will prove victorious over the foreigners, albeit only after a long and painful struggle.

Y Ddraig Goch is only one of a number of dragon-like beasts to prowl their way through Welsh folklore. Elsewhere in the *Mabinogion* there is a tale of the knight Peredur, who slays a huge and hideous serpent on whose tail is fixed a ring of gold. Peredur claims the ring for himself – shades of Tolkien here! Peredur, King Arthur and an even more ancient superhero, *Hu Gadarn* ('Hugh the Mighty') are all credited with the destruction of a water monster called the *Afanc*.

The Welsh flag proudly bears the emblem of Y Ddraig Goch, the Red Dragon.

Although it is generally referred to as the *Afanc* singular, each story may refer to a different creature. They are of indeterminate appearance and inhabited more than one lake. One thing they had in common: they were enormously powerful. In the oldest story, the *Afanc* lurked in a now unidentified and possibly mythical lake called Llyn Llion. Its thrashing about in the water caused terrible floods which regularly drowned the country round about. *Hu Gadarn* employed the two gigantic oxen called the *Ychen Bannog* to drag out the fearsome monster, which he then killed. The strain of removing the *Afanc* caused one of the oxen to die, and the other wandered off, mournfully lowing for his fallen comrade. The bard Iolo Morganwg locates this adventure to the area around Llanddewi Brefi in Ceredigion.

In a later source, it is the heroic Arthur who drags the *Afanc* from its watery lair, in this case Llyn Barfog (Bearded Lake), near Aberdyfi. The beast has also been associated with Llangorse Lake (Llyn Syfaddon) near Brecon and Llyn yr Afanc near Betws y Coed. It should be noted, however, that *afanc* is the word for 'beaver' in modern Welsh and the latter may simply be named after this harmless furry critter, which lived in Wales for centuries.

The author Marie Trevelyan collected many folk stories from friends, neighbours, servants and travelling tinkers as well as from a number of more scholarly sources. In her 1909 book *Folk-Lore and Folk Stories of Wales,* she relates an interesting encounter with another water monster, this time in Bala Lake (Llyn Tegid). She writes: 'It was said Bala Lake was bottomless. Centuries ago an expert diver tried it, but was terribly frightened by his experience. He asserted that a dragon was coiled up at the bottom of the lake, and if he had not been very careful the creature would have swallowed him.'

Oddly enough, there are much more recent accounts of something huge and unidentified being seen swimming in Bala Lake. I spoke to one of the witnesses myself, a no-nonsense angler who had fished the lake for many years previously. Despite the ridicule he received, he refused to back down from his glimpse of an enormous animal just below the surface of the water. I for one believe him. The creature was nicknamed 'Teggie' by the Press in acknowledgement of its famous Scottish cousin in Loch Ness.

In the 18th century there was a report of a monster in Llyn y Gader, a small lake below Mount Snowdon. A man was attempting to swim the lake when his friends by the shore spied a 'long, trailing object' approaching him on the surface. Just as the swimmer was reaching the opposite shore, the head of some colossal serpent emerged from the water and it threw its coils around him. The poor man was dragged under and devoured before anyone could do anything to help.

Bala Lake (Llyn Tegid) was said to be the home of an aquatic monster – and may be still!

Marie Trevelyan lists a wide range of places supposedly infested at one time by 'lesser dragons and winged serpents'. They include: the Llŷn Peninsula, Cader Idris, Plinlimmon, the Brecon Beacons, Worm's Head in Gower, 'the marshes of Carmarthen' and 'the ravines of the Berwyn Mountains'.

Perhaps the most interesting habitat Trevelyan learnt of was the woodland round Penllyn Castle, near Bridgend in South Wales. An 'aged inhabitant' told her that his father and uncle had often killed winged serpents in the woods because they were 'as bad as foxes for poultry'. He described them as being vividly coloured, 'as though they were covered with jewels of all sorts', and some had crests which sparkled with all the colours of the rainbow. Similar flying serpents, though not so brightly coloured, were rumoured to have thrived elsewhere in the Vale of Glamorgan, in woods at Penmark and Beaupre.

Waterfalls were also favourite resorts of dragons in bygone Wales. Several waterfalls in the Vale of Neath were haunted by them, particularly those of the rivers Hepste, Mellte and Perddyn. They were also seen flying around falls at Erwyd, Resolven and Ystradgynlais.

A particularly unpleasant example of the breed lived in a cavern behind Wales's highest waterfall, at Llanrhaeadr ym Mochnant in northern Powys. It was a deadly menace to the entire district, leaving its lair to swoop on livestock and people, too. Eventually a *Dyn Hysbys* was consulted. He instructed the people to set up a pillar of stone and fix into it numerous sharp iron spikes. Then they were to drape it in a red cloth and, when the dragon was on the wing, light a bonfire beneath it. This they did and the monster, on seeing it, became enraged, believing the fiery red pillar to be a rival dragon. It hurled itself onto the stone in a fury of teeth and talons – and tore itself apart on the spikes concealed beneath the cloth. The pillar can still be seen: a tall prehistoric standing stone. It is known by two names: Post Coch ('Red Pillar') and Post y Wiber ('Pillar of the Serpent').

A terrible flying dragon had its lair at Pistyll Rhaeadr, the highest waterfall in Wales.

IStock Photo

DEVILISH DOINGS

One of the best-known legends from Wales is told about the so-called 'Devil's Bridge' in Ceredigion. The 'bridge' is actually three bridges, all spanning a ravine through which tumbles the Mynach river, before joining the River Rheidol 300 feet (90m) below. Mynach means 'monk' and it's likely the lowest and oldest bridge was built for the use of monks. It was constructed in the 11th century, a single narrow arch perched precariously, as it seems, over the falls. The nearby village of Pontarfynach ('Bridge on the Monk') is named after this original bridge.

In the 18th century a wider and longer span was built above the medieval bridge. The builders used the original bridge to erect the scaffolding during the new one's construction – which just goes to show how solid a structure it really is. A 20th-century bridge now spans the two historical ones. But it is the original bridge which interests us here. Its construction in such a remote and difficult place suggested the idea that only the Devil himself could have built it.

According to the legend, as retold by W. Jenkyn Thomas in his *Welsh Fairy Book* (1907), a poor woman named Megan was standing on one side of the ravine in great distress of mind because her only cow had somehow found its way to the other side. It seemed impossible: it must have wandered miles out of its way in order to find anywhere to cross the river, but the fact remained that there it was, quietly chewing the cud on a patch of grass high above the falls.

IStock Photo

The Devil's Bridge at Pontarfynach from a Victorian engraving.

'Oh dear, oh dear, what shall I do?' cried poor Megan. Then she heard a calm voice behind her: 'What is the matter, Megan?' The voice belonged to a monk. Megan jumped, because she had not heard him approach. She explained her predicament to the stranger and out of the depths of his cowl his soothing voice spoke again. 'I'll get her back for you,' he said, and went on to say that it was an 'amusement' of his to build bridges and that he would be delighted to do so now. Megan thought the monk must be joking and pointed out that the cow was the only wealth she had in the world: how could she possibly pay him for such a service?

'I'm very easily satisfied,' said the monk. 'Just let me have the first living thing that crosses the bridge and I shall be content.'

Megan agreed to this and the monk told her to return to her cottage while he got on with his work. Now, Megan was long enough in the tooth to realise that this was all too good to be true and there had to be a catch somewhere. She was unable to see the monk's face in the shadow of his deep cowl, but as she squeezed past him on the narrow path, she did happen to glimpse his foot where it peeped out from beneath the hem of his habit. There was something very unusual about that little black foot – it was a hoof! Realising she had literally done a deal with the Devil, Megan sat at home trying to come up with a plan to foil whatever scheme the Evil One was plotting.

When the call came, Megan returned to find the 'monk' proudly displaying a stone arch over the chasm. She guessed that the Devil was intending to trick her into crossing over the newly built bridge, so that he could claim her soul. So she played for time. She pretended to be unimpressed.

'Is it strong?' she asked. 'Will it hold the weight of this loaf?' She produced a freshly baked loaf from under her shawl.

Megan defeats the fiendish monk at Devil's Bridge. Illustration by Willy Pogany from The Welsh Fairy Book.

'Hold the weight of this loaf? Throw it on and see,' replied the Devil, annoyed by the old woman's lack of respect for his work. Unnoticed by the Evil One, Megan had been surreptitiously tearing off bits of the loaf every few yards or so as she walked from her cottage to the ravine. Her little dog had soon found these morsels and was following Megan, snapping them up. Now Megan rolled the loaf across the Devil's Bridge and the dog scampered after it.

> *'Yes, it will do,' said Megan, 'and, kind sir, my little dog is the first live thing to cross the bridge. You are welcome to him, and I thank you very much for the trouble you have taken.'*

'Tut, the silly dog is no good to me,' complained the so-called monk and he vanished in a cloud of brimstone, convincing Megan of his fiendish nature and that she had had a lucky escape. Not only that, but she now had a handy bridge for her use, and the first thing she did was to cross it and bring her straying cow and her little dog home.

The Devil (*Y Diawl*) appears in many similar tales to the one above. His Satanic Majesty is rarely portrayed as anything other than a buffoon, capable of being outwitted by any crafty Welsh man or woman. The medieval poet, Sion Kent, for example, is said to have sold his soul to the Devil for fame and fortune. A condition in the contract stated that the Devil would claim him whether or not his body was buried in consecrated ground. Sion defeated this clause by having himself buried under the churchyard wall – neither in, nor outside, the consecrated space. Another folk hero, Sion Dafydd, outwits Satan on numerous occasions. In one adventure, he offers the Devil a smoke of his pipe, but it is really a pistol, and he shoots the Devil through the head.

A story is told in many parts of Wales of a mysterious stranger turning up at a house where men are at play with cards. He joins the game. At first, he loses hand after hand, his debts rising. But then he ups the stakes, suggesting the men play for their souls instead of money. It is then that someone notices his cloven hoofs and, thus exposed, he vanishes in a rage up the chimney. In these stories, there is no need to even outwit the Devil: all it takes to get rid of him is to recognise his true identity and to cross oneself or offer up a prayer.

In some of these stories, the Devil's other role is to frighten people who have been sinning, especially if they have been failing to go to church on a Sunday. Sabbath-breakers (as they were known) might be going about entirely innocent pursuits, as we would view them today, but this would not save them from the Evil One's attentions. A person who skipped church to gather nuts one morning in Denbighshire, for example, was terrified by a huge, hairy arm which pushed its way through the nut-bush and made

The Devil and a good wizard fight over the soul of a hapless young Welshman in another illustration by Willy Pogany.

to grab them. Boys playing football on a Sunday in Caerphilly also received an unwelcome visit from the Devil.

As Elias Owen points out, it's peculiar that Satan himself should frighten sinners into remission, since this would have been somewhat contrary to his own interests. Owen retells a particularly good example of this sort of yarn in his *Welsh Folklore*. In this case, the Sabbath-breaker appears to have been tempted by the Devil in disguise but it his foolish oath which dooms him:

'About half a mile from Cynwyd [near Corwen] is the "Mill Waterfall", beneath which is a deep whirlpool, where a man, who was fishing there on Sunday, once found an enormous fish. "I will catch him though the Devil take me," said the presumptuous man. The fish went under the fall, the man followed him, and was never afterwards seen.'

THE FEAR OF WITCHCRAFT

Once upon a time, and for many centuries, it was believed that misfortune, illness and even death could be willed upon a person by another skilled in mystic arts or who had been given the power to do so by the Devil. Because witchcraft appears in the Bible (for example, in the story of the Witch of Endor and the conjuring up of a demon for King Solomon), the 'dark arts' were believed in as firmly by educated people as the illiterate. King James VI of Scotland (later James I of England), for example, was a firm believer in witchcraft and was convinced there had been several plots made against him by witches and sorcerers.

It might seem the height of foolish ignorance to believe in witchcraft but it should be remembered that prior to the 18th century almost nothing was understood about the causes of disease. Microbes were unknown. Although you have never seen the virus that infects you with the common cold, you believe in it to the same extent as your ancestors did the witches they were told existed in their communities.

So firm was the belief in witchcraft that someone accused of cursing an animal or human to fall ill or die was treated just the same as if they had poisoned or murdered their victims by more orthodox means. The criminal justice system saw no difference: the end result was all that mattered. By the dawn of the 17th century, however, Europe had fallen into the grip of a 'witch mania', fuelled in part by the resurgence of bubonic plague and by religious insecurity fanned by the Renaissance. No one was safe from being accused of being a witch. Lonely old women, especially those who had previously been known to provide herbal remedies, harmless love charms and the like, were early targets, but even the nobility found themselves accused, often by the unscrupulous as a means to get them out of the way.

Thousands of supposed witches and male sorcerers were hanged or burned alive as the mania swept Europe. Aside from a number of high-profile cases, and the reprehensible campaign by the sadistic conman Matthew Hopkins, the self-styled 'Witchfinder General' of East Anglia, the British Isles escaped the worst effects of this paranoia. Wales probably suffered least. In some remote rural districts the belief in witches lingered longer, however, leading to a few startling court cases well into the 19th century.

One of the most shocking I have come across took place in Monmouthshire in the 1820s. A farmer who believed his cattle had been bewitched dragged a very elderly woman from her home and began to commit all sorts of assaults upon her in a bid to remove the supposed curse. This included dragging thorns across her skin in order to make her bleed. It was a long-standing belief that drawing blood could rob a witch of her power. Joining in with this brutality were two farm-hands and, disgracefully, a police constable. All four stripped the poor woman – who was in her nineties – to her waist so that they could look for 'witch marks' on her flesh which they said would indicate where she had suckled demons! They hacked off her hair for the same bizarre purpose.

By this time a crowd of jeering onlookers had gathered. They egged on the four assailants to drag their victim off to a pond, where they could 'duck' her. Ducking was an old method to try a witch – the accused was thrown into a body of water and if she floated it proved she had supernatural powers. If she sank, she would be presumed innocent but had probably drowned by the time the mob's verdict had been reached. Fortunately, the Monmouthshire mob was prevented from carrying out this callous scheme by the intervention of the woman's daughter.

This intervention was as fortunate for them as it was for their elderly victim. If they had gone through with it, they may have found themselves on a charge of murder. When, in due course, the ringleaders found themselves in court, the chairman of the magistrates lamented that 'the prisoners had acted under a delusion founded on superstition … and he regretted that there was anyone in the kingdom who should have been so deploringly ignorant as to have fallen into such an error'.

IStock Photo

A ducking stool, used to determine whether or not a woman was a witch. An elderly Monmouthshire woman accused of witchcraft in the 19th century narrowly escaped a ducking by a mob.

SOME WELSH WITCHES

Although the witch mania that swept Europe in the 17th century had largely run out of steam by the time it reached as far west as Wales, there remains nonetheless a great deal of Welsh folklore devoted to alleged witches.

Among the most notorious were the witches of Llanddona, on Anglesey. They were a group of men and women who washed ashore on the north coast of the island, more dead than alive, having been expelled from their (unspecified) homeland for practising the dark arts. As soon as they had recovered, they lost no time in setting up home and terrorising the locals. The women begged from door to door, threatening to curse anyone who failed to give them food. If they bid for anything at the markets, there would be no other bidders, for any animal purchased after outbidding them was sure to die within days.

The men made their money through smuggling, but they too had recourse to witchcraft. They had the control of a familiar spirit that took the form of a fly. If they found themselves hard pressed by revenue men, the smugglers would release the fly and it would immediately buzz into the eyes of the officers, blinding them. The smugglers could then make their escape.

In Pembrokeshire, witches were said to have come from Flanders in Belgium, riding to South West Wales on cockle shells. Numerous people came to Pembrokeshire from Flanders in the Middle Ages to join the weaving trade, and this tradition suggests they were treated with considerable suspicion. For some reason I admit I can't fathom, tailors in old Glamorganshire had the reputation of being able to bewitch people and were also regarded with suspicion.

Elsewhere in Glamorgan, witches had the reputation of being able to turn themselves into foxes. They would do so in order to baffle the hounds during foxhunts. In the neighbourhood of Porthcawl, an old witch was said to be able to transform into the shape of a grey goose. The goose would often appear to put those hunting rabbits or wildfowl off their shots. These examples are variants of more common stories, told throughout the British Isles, of witches transforming themselves into cats or hares.

IStock Photo

Witches at their revels. Such fanciful illustrations helped to fuel the fear felt by peasantry and nobles alike of the reality of the power of witchcraft.

A particularly unusual witch was recorded in the parish of Llangynfelyn, in Ceredigion. Her story appears in a 1930s book called *Coelion Cymru* ('Superstitions of the Welsh') by Evan Isaac. The book is in Welsh and I am grateful to my friend Rosie Smith for translating the following passage. According to Isaac, the witch lived in a swamp and was responsible for spreading the disease which today we call malaria:

'Local folk believed the marsh was her home and that within it she was all-knowing and all-powerful. She never left her home except in the dead of night in thick fog because she was ashamed of her ugliness; luckily for her there was plenty of fog around the marsh.

'Betsen of Llain Fanadl met her once. Betsen lived in a cottage on the edge of the marsh, and one evening as she returned from collecting firewood she saw a woman sitting on a hump of sedge. The woman had a large head, and jet black hair that fell in a huge wave down her back and piled up on the floor; she was eating buckbeans and frog meat. Betsen called out: "Good evening." The witch jumped up, and Betsen saw she was seven feet tall, thin, bony and sallow, with black teeth. The witch hissed like a snake in Betsen's face, then disappeared. Betsen was said never to be the same again.

'The residents of Taliesin were troubled for generations by a disease, a type of fever, and the symptoms were particularly bad in some people. At first they felt weak and ill as though they were seasick. Then their whole body would start shaking, which would last a full hour. They would shake once a day, but one hour later each time. This would continue for eight to ten days. The disease was believed to be caused by the witch, and it was named after her. On dark nights she made a thick fog, crept in it to the village, sneaked into the house of her choice despite any efforts to prevent her, and into the bedroom, then breathed her curse on the sleepers. They would wake the next morning from a restless sleep full of bad spirits, feeling ill and depressed. Shaking would begin later that day.'

IStock Photo

The typical view of the wicked witch, riding on her broomstick to the sabbat. Her outfit is oddly reminiscent of traditional Welsh dress.

The disease, which the people referred to as *y Grwach Hen* or 'the Old Witch', ceased after the people of the parish began to use coal instead of peat to heat their homes. This meant they no longer needed to go so often into the marsh, where, unbeknownst to them, they were being bitten by malaria-carrying mosquitoes.

The description of the witch and her fondness for lurking in damp, foggy places identifies her as a weird entity called the *Gwrach y Rhibyn,* which translates as something like 'Witch (or Hag) of the Damp Mists'. *Rhibyn* has no direct translation in English, but usually refers to the all-encompassing drizzly fog that has a habit of descending on Welsh mountain-tops. Another of these hags had her home in a bog that had originally formed part of the moat round Caerphilly Castle. She had a habit of rising out of the bog, moaning and groaning. The nearby residents got so fed up with her that the men and boys tried to catch her in a net, but failed.

Fairies, witches and ghosts are often indistinguishable in Welsh folklore – they are all *ellyllon* or *bwganod,* both words meaning goblins or spooks.

HEALING MAGIC

The reverse of the medal to the traditions and phobias regarding witchcraft is a long tradition of what is popularly called 'white magic' performed by so-called wise men and women in rural communities. These people were more or less skilled in herbalism and drew up charms and spells based on biblical and earlier sources. Their charms might be drawn up to repel the dark arts of malicious witches; to further a love interest; or to find lost or stolen goods. Some wise men were held in such awe that a thief would confess rather than suffer the results of their magic. Many wise women were also midwives. Tragically, these good women were among the first people to find themselves accused during the witch hunts.

I unearthed many examples of folk medicine practiced in Wales while researching the contents of a journal called *Bye-gones,* published between 1871 and 1939. A correspondent from Wrexham, for example, wrote in with information about a local character, Ned Edwards, a carriage driver. Every morning, just after sun-up, Ned would forage for snails in the dewy grass in Eagles Meadow. Only snails with white shells would do. Ned would swallow them, 'all alive and kicking', as he put it, shells and all. He did this to ward off tuberculosis, a common disease in his day and usually fatal. Ned had adopted this bizarre dose of self-medication in his youth and was in his ripe old age by the time of his mention in *Bye-gones,* so perhaps there was something in it.

Snails also came in handy as wart-removers. Again, it was important to gather them at dawn. After being rubbed on each wart in turn, they would then be pinned on the thorns of hawthorn bushes and left to die. It was believed the warts would fade away as the snails rotted. This concept of transmitting a disease to an unfortunate animal was a universal one. A muslin bag full of spiders hung around the neck was thought to cure whooping cough: as the spiders died, so would the disease. The old Welsh name for shingles is *eryri* (which means 'eagles') and in Wales it was believed that anyone who had consumed the flesh of an eagle would be able to cure the rash by spreading their saliva on it. Similarly, a person who had eaten the flesh of a crow could cure croup, presumably because this illness made one croak like a crow.

In Llandegla, in Denbighshire, there was a thriving trade in 'cures' for epilepsy. Poultry were kept by the churchwarden for the express purpose of having the epilepsy transmitted to them in an elaborate ritual which involved the afflicted sleeping on the altar of St Tegla's Church with his chosen fowl beside him in a basket. Needless to say, a fee was charged for the rent of each bird.

IStock Photo

The humble snail was used in a number of ways in Welsh folk medicine. Ned the Cab Driver believed white-shelled snails were especially efficacious.

Holy ground had an allure of its own in the days before modern medicine. Grass from the churchyard was believed to cure rabies, and grease wiped from the church bells (called 'bell breech') was considered sovereign in clearing up ringworm, piles and an alarming condition called 'wild warts'. Death itself could be employed to enhance life. Moss which had grown on a graveyard skull was said to ease headaches if dried, powdered and taken like snuff. The hand of a dead man, especially a suicide, was supposed to be able to remove tumours and other swellings if stroked across the offending part. A spoonful of earth from the grave of a recently interred virgin dissolved in water was said to cure tuberculosis.

A certain amount of ritual seems to have added to the supposed effect of some of these remedies. Studies by anthropologists have shown that elaborate ritual can lead to a state of mind in which the subconscious can perform many surprising things, including healing. In our society, hypnotism can produce a similar effect, and the power of a placebo, a sugar pill containing no medicine but resulting in a cure nonetheless, is well known. It is possible, therefore, that if a patient really believes that even the most unlikely ingredient or practice will cure him, it might well do so. This would be one reason why so many folk remedies continued to be used for so long.

Arguably the most extraordinary description of white witchcraft in action also came from the periodical *Bye-gones*. In the edition of 10 April 1901, a correspondent calling himself 'W.A.R.' describes a folk remedy carried out on a man with toothache and another on a person suffering from whitlow, a painful swelling of the tips of the fingers caused by infection from a herpes virus. In both accounts, we learn of the existence of the *pryf* as the cause of the ailment. In modern Welsh *pryf* translates as 'insect' but, as will become apparent, this is not an accurate way to describe the weird thing supposedly extracted by the healer. Of course, in colloquial English, people often say they 'have a bug' when feeling unwell, and this may also hark back to a time before we knew about bacteria and viruses. Thanks to 'W.A.R.' we have an excellent description of a ritual performed to remove the *pryf*.

'I remember some years ago being in the company of an old man, a native of Anglesey, since dead,' writes the correspondent. 'In the course of conversation he stated that he well recollected going in his younger days with a farm labourer, who was suffering intensely from toothache, to an elderly woman in Anglesey, who, he said, was locally noted for her ability to cure this affliction. The sufferer was released from his torture, and "never afterwards suffered from toothache". I asked the old man if he could describe the process by which the cure was supposed to have been effected.

'He told me that the woman first took a round piece of iron, hollowed out in the middle, and placed it in the fire until it became red hot. This was taken out, and in the hollow she placed a handful of seeds (my informant telling me it resembled carrot seed), and over all was inverted an earthenware jar. After waiting some time the woman took up the jar, which was now found to be blackened on the inside. Boiling water was poured into it, and the sufferer from toothache had to place his face over the jar and inhale the steam.

'My informant added that before they left the cottage, the old woman took a needle and pricked from the surface of the water in the jar a minute speck, which she asserted was the *pryf*, which was the cause of the toothache.'

In relation to the soreness on the hands, 'W.A.R.' also recalled overhearing an elderly woman in Gwynedd describing the extraction of the *pryf* from her husband's finger. She told her friend she had seen it with her own eyes and that it was 'something like a centipede'. She saw it crawling on the table before the healer killed it.

A wise woman sets about manufacturing her herbal remedies.

HEROES AND SAINTS

Legends of King Arthur exist all over the British Isles but Wales arguably has the best claim to him. The oldest surviving manuscripts mentioning the legendary hero are Welsh in origin and it's worth recalling that although he is thought of as having been 'king of Britain' or 'of the Britons', the sources actually state *Prydain,* the Welsh name that has since been anglicised to 'Britain'. Modern Britons are largely unaware that the terms 'Briton' and 'British' were originally synonymous with 'Welsh'.

Arthur features in many of the early folk tales collected as the *Mabinogion* by Lady Charlotte Guest. He has many adventures throughout the Welsh countryside. We have already learnt of his fight to drag a monster out of Llyn Barfog, beside which his horse left a permanent imprint in a rock. A similar imprint can be found on an old stone on the border between Flintshire and Denbighshire. It is called Carreg Carn March Arthur, or 'Stone of the Hoof of Arthur's Horse'. In one of the stories, Arthur leads an epic hunt for a monstrous boar called *Twrch Trwyth* ('Trwyth the Boar'). During the nationwide chase after the brute, Arthur's dog, Cafall, left his pawprint in a stone on a mountain near Builth Wells. Arthur was so struck by this phenomenon that he built a cairn on the summit, topped off with the magically impressed stone. The cairn still bears the name Carn Cafall in honour of the hound.

Numerous places are named after the hero. Several present Arthur as a giant in more than just reputation. A prehistoric chambered tomb on Anglesey bears the name, in English, of Arthur's Quoits.

Quoits was a popular game once upon a time in which stones or horseshoes are thrown at a target. For Arthur to have used the massive capstone of the tomb as a quoit demonstrates his enormous strength. The story attached to Arthur's Stone on the Gower makes his gigantic stature more overt. The stone – another ancient burial chamber – is said to have found its way into Arthur's shoe as he was striding through the country on his way to his showdown at the Battle of Camlann. Irritated by the 'pebble', the king removed it and threw it away. It landed where it still resides, on Cefn y Bryn.

A more recent Welsh hero, Owain Glyndwr, has also, literally, left his mark on Welsh folklore. In 1400 Glyndwr spearheaded a revolt in Wales, striking out across the nation and capturing or burning castles. The Lords of March and the Earl of Northumberland originally agreed to help him overthrow the English king and carve up England and Wales between them, but they ultimately let him down. Promising talks with the Irish and Bretons also fell through and by 1409 the rebellion had been quashed. Owain was never captured, however. His ghost is said to have appeared at Valle Crucis Abbey near Llangollen, so perhaps he was buried there. A stone on a hillside above Corwen bears a fairly convincing imprint of a shoe and tradition states this as belonging to Owain Glyndwr, granting him true supernatural hero status.

The early Welsh saints were a force to be reckoned with, too. Two saints active in North Wales during the Dark Ages put paid to a tyrant named *Benlli Gawr* ('Benlli the Giant'). According to tradition, Benlli attacked the settlement at Yr Wyddgrug, now also called Mold, with a host of Pictish mercenaries. Warned of his approach, the local holy man, St Garmon, organised the men of the community to hide around the slopes of a hollow in the land through which Benlli's army was sure to pass. They

Arthur's Stone on the Gower – a 'pebble' in the shoe of the legendary king.

IStock Photo

had few weapons and couldn't hope to fight off the invaders, so St Garmon was forced to come up with a cunning plan. When Benlli and his mercenaries had marched halfway through the field, St Garmon and his men leapt up, brandishing ploughshares and other makeshift weapons, and in unison they cried out: 'Alleluia!'

The result was so startling that the Picts believed they were being ambushed by a much stronger force than was the case and they fled back the way they had come. They probably hadn't anticipated any resistance at all. Afterwards, this adventure became known as the 'Alleluia Battle'. The place where it is said to have occurred has long borne the name Maes Garmon, or 'Garmon's Field'.

St Garmon (who has been identified with Germanus of Auxerre, a French missionary) had not finished with *Benlli Gawr*. Sometime later, he made his way up to Benlli's fortress on top of the mountain still named after him, Moel Fenlli in the Clwydian Range. His hope was to convert Benlli and his unruly court to Christianity and a better way of living, but he was refused entry. As an insult to the holy man, Benlli sent his lowliest servant, a swineherd named Cadell, to send him away. Cadell was the only decent man in the court. He took St Garmon to stay the night in his shack and killed a calf, one of only two animals he owned, to feed him.

The following morning Cadell was amazed to find that the calf he had slaughtered the night before was alive and whole again and quietly feeding beside its mother. St Garmon was at his devotions. At length, he rose from his knees and quietly suggested that his humble host not go into the fortress that day. Then he returned to Yr Wyddgrug. Shortly afterwards a fireball dropped from the sky and destroyed the fortress and everyone inside. Cadell was the only survivor of Benlli's court and went on to become a noble ruler.

St Winefride's Well at Holywell (Treffynnon) in Flintshire came into being through an act of violence and a subsequent miracle. Winefride was a pious, pure-hearted virgin who one morning attracted the unwelcome attention of a passing nobleman. Her beauty inflamed his lust and, despite her protestations that she had promised herself to God, he tried to ravish the girl. She struggled so fiercely that he finally let her go, but in a rage at being spurned, her drew his sword and hacked off her head. He ran off, just as Winefride's uncle, St Beuno, came on the scene. St Beuno reverently re-attached Winefride's head to her neck and she came to life again. Where she had fallen, a spring of clear water gushed forth. This spring became St Winefride's Well, still resorted to today by the faithful hoping for miraculous cures.

Two other virgins with a special place in Welsh hagiography and folklore are the saints Dwynwen and Melangell. Dwynwen lived on Anglesey. She was in love with a young man named Maelon but, having given herself to God, refused to marry him. A tragic series of events, dependent on what version of the story you read, followed this refusal. Ultimately, Dwynwen is granted three wishes by an angel: that she should never be forced to marry, that Maelon should live happily without her and that God should 'look after all true lovers'. She then retired to a hermit's cell on Ynys Llanddwyn, the island named after her, where a medieval cult built up around her memory. St Dwynwen continues to be thought of as the Welsh equivalent of St Valentine.

Melangell was a similarly religious-minded girl who had a particular affinity for all the animals living in the valley in Mid Wales where she lived. One day, while she was at prayer, a hare came racing up to her. She caught it and then hid it in her gown when she saw the reason for its flight: it was being pursued by a huntsman and his hounds. This was no ordinary huntsman: it was Brochwel

The site of St Dwynwen's hermitage on the beautiful little island of Llanddwyn just off the western coast of Anglesey.

IStock Photo

Yscythrog, the Prince of Powys. He demanded that Melangell give up the hare but she refused. She faced down his snarling hounds and they retreated, whimpering. Brochwel realised he was in the presence of someone extraordinary. After long conversation, Brochwel gave to Melangell land throughout the valley, where she founded a nunnery given over to quiet contemplation. The valley is now named Pennant Melangell and the church is dedicated to her. For centuries, hares here were nicknamed *Oen Melangell*, 'Melangell's Lambs'.

Perhaps not surprisingly, Wales's patron saint, St David or Dewi Sant, is the one with the greatest reputation for remarkable deeds. Even before he was born, he was showing off. When a preacher began declaiming to his virgin but pregnant mother in an offensive manner, the foetal David struck him dumb. As a child, he was taught his lessons by a talking dove with a golden beak. He grew to be a man of 'gigantic stature and fabulous beauty' and magical events took place around him almost casually.

At Llanddewi Brefi (named after him), in Ceredigion, the flat field on which he was delivering a sermon suddenly bulged up into a mound so that the people could see and hear him better. One summer's day, he was walking across the countryside and became terribly thirsty under the hot sun. At a place called Glyn Hodnant, he sat down and a cooling spring – not of water but of fine wine – immediately burst out of the ground beside him. On another occasion he was seen to absent-mindedly hang his hat on a sunbeam. Other incidents were far more dramatic: raising a drowned child from the dead, freezing the hand of a man about to strike another with an axe, and blasting a host of wicked wizards with fire from heaven. Finally, St David chose the date of his own death (1 March), having decided at the advanced age of 147 that it was time to go.

OMENS OF DEATH

One of the more unusual miracles attributed to St David was the instigation of signs and portents that would warn good Christian Welsh men and women of their approaching death. St David supposedly petitioned God that his brethren should be given a warning so that they would have plenty of time to see to the health of their souls. Together these death omens are known in Welsh as *tolaeth,* a word of uncertain derivation possibly referring to the tolling of a bell or, more likely, related to the word for 'family', *teulu,* since these are very personal spooks.

At one time the Welsh seem to have been morbidly concerned with these portents and there is a seemingly endless roster of them. Mysterious knocks and taps were commonly thought to warn of a coming death and were often reported as being heard in the rooms of dying people. Carpenters would sometimes claim to have heard the sounds of sawing and nailing in their workshops the night before someone came to order a coffin. One night, near Porthcawl, a visitor to an inn distinctly heard the sounds of heavy breathing and the scuffling of feet in the parlour, the night before a group of fishermen carried in the body of a drowned colleague: the sounds they made in doing so correlating with those the witness had previously heard.

Even stranger was the *aderyn corff* or 'corpse bird', which would flap against the window of a room where anyone lay dying. A Pembrokeshire woman, Miss Griffiths, told folklorist John Ceredig Davies that she saw the *aderyn corff* fluttering at the window just before her father died. She described the bird as 'a little grey one'. Even the humble chicken could once spell doom in Wales. A hen laying two eggs in the same day was a sign of death; the laying of an unusually small egg was also unlucky.

Similar beliefs are traceable in the other Celtic countries, but less so in England. Most people are familiar with the 'banshee' of Ireland. This was a spirit, often attached to a particular family, that would wail mournfully in the days leading up to a family member's death. On the rare occasions a banshee was seen, it appeared as a grim old hag dressed in rags. The Welsh had a version of the banshee, too – or rather, two versions. If the wailing warning of misfortune was no more than a disembodied voice, it was known as the *Cyhiraeth*. Sometimes an apparition was seen, however – in the form of a creature even more ghastly to look upon than her Irish equivalent. This spirit was known as the *Gwrach y Rhibyn*, or (roughly translated) 'hag of the mists'. We have encountered a close cousin of this phantom in the 'Some Welsh Witches' chapter.

We have an excellent description of the *Gwrach y Rhibyn* from a man who claimed to have seen it at Llandaff. The witness stated that one night in November 1877, he was awoken by 'a frightful screeching and a shaking of my window'. He jumped out of bed and took a look outside. He writes:

'Then I saw the *Gwrach y Rhibyn* ... a horrible old woman with long red hair and a face like chalk, and great teeth like tusks, looking back over her shoulder at me as she went through the air with a long black gown trailing along the ground below her arms, for body I could make out none. She gave another unearthly screech while I looked at her; then I heard her flapping her wings against the window of the house just below the one I was in, and she vanished from my sight.'

An old illustration of the Irish banshee, whose characteristics are almost identical to the less well-known Welsh equivalent, the Gwrach y Rhibyn.

The next morning he learnt that a man in the house where the apparition had been flapping its wings had died during the night.

The *tolaeth* proper was a phantom in the form of a funeral procession. This portent took two forms: either the shadowy spectre of the cortege, or the sounds of one. In either case it would prove a warning of a real funeral shortly to occur in the community and, in the case of a visual apparition, resemble in every way the procession that was soon to take place. The phantom would follow the route soon to be taken by the cortege and the witness to it would have no difficulty in recognising details such as the faces of the mourners.

In parts of South Wales the phenomena were known as 'fairy funerals' because it was believed the appearance was created by the fairies as a warning to the neighbourhood. The *tolaeth* could be quite dangerous. After dark, many superstitious people would only walk along the sides of some lanes, rather than down the middle, in case they encountered a phantom funeral – there are tales of people being trodden underfoot by the relentless tread of the ghostly mourners.

There are scores of examples from Wales. In her *Folk-Lore and Folk Stories of Wales* (1909), Marie Trevelyan highlights an old chapel at Bethesda'r Fro, in the Vale of Glamorgan, which had a reputation for manifestations of this phenomenon. A dramatic example was told to her by an old lady.

One evening in 1871, the witness saw dim lights burning in the chapel at Bethesda and she then noticed a crowd was approaching. A moment later she found herself jostled 'unmercifully' by a mass of mourners. The woman struggled to get through them, eventually reaching the chapel gates. But her adventure was far from over, for here she was startled by the sight of a huge white dog chasing after a piebald pony, which was kicking and rearing in terror. The crowd surged back out of the frantic pony's way, and the woman took advantage of the sudden gap to make her escape, running as fast as she could past the chapel. She was horrified, however, to feel stones hurled after her as she did so. By the time she reached her friends' house at Boverton, she was so overcome by her experience that she fainted.

Naturally she told all her friends about her experience, and the details were so striking that they remembered them three weeks later when they were all called upon to attend a funeral at Bethesda. Everything occurred exactly as the witness had previously experienced it. A big white dog snapped at a piebald pony, sending it careering through the crowd, scattering some newly laid stones as it did so. The stones hit the woman.

A young woman watches in dread as a phantom funeral passes along a country lane.

Rivalling the phantom funerals for their frequency are the other major example of the *tolaeth*, the 'corpse candles', or *canwyllau cyrff*. Belief in corpse candles was very widespread in Wales and many sober-minded people claimed to have seen them. Elias Owen, in his *Welsh Folklore* of 1896, describes the phenomenon in this manner: 'The corpse candle … was a light like that of a candle, which was said to issue from the house where a death was about to occur, and take the course of the funeral procession to the burial place. This was the usual way of proceeding, but this mysterious light was also said to wend its way to the abode of a person about to die.'

When the grandly named W.Y. Evans-Wentz was researching his *Fairy Faith in Celtic Countries*, he interviewed an old lady of Pembrokeshire who told him she had seen a corpse candle 'right here in the very room where we are sitting and talking' (she lived in a cottage a stone's throw away from one of Wales's most spectacular ancient monuments, the Pentre Ifan cromlech). She described the *canwyll corff* as 'a luminous mass, lightish blue in colour'. Shortly after her experience, a member of her family passed away.

One of the most interesting stories regarding a corpse candle in Wales appeared in one of the first 'penny dreadful' magazines, published during the Georgian period, the *Terrific Register*. Historian Cate Ludlow has been editing compilations from the *Terrific Register* and similar publications for the History Press and I am grateful to her for drawing my attention to it. According to this yarn, which was printed in 1825, the appearance of a *canwyll corff* helped to expose a murder.

'A farmer happening to be overtaken by a violent storm of hail and rain, near the hut of a poor labourer, who lived not far from Rhytwin in North Wales, stopped at it, in order to take shelter,' states the account. 'The storm continuing, the labourer offered the farmer a bed, which the latter, being very much fatigued, gladly accepted. No sooner was the farmer fast asleep, but the labourer, who conjectured that he must have a considerable sum of money about him, murdered his guest, and taking the money, which amounted to twenty pounds, buried the body on rising ground behind the hut; and early the next morning went off to Bristol.

'The hut was soon after taken by another labourer, who late in the evening observed a light, which settled constantly on the same spot on the eminence; sometimes there appeared two together, which after blazing a considerable time, suddenly disappeared, and left him filled with terror and consternation. He apprehended that this appearance signified that he was soon to die, and in the anxiety of mind, he imparted what he had seen to three of his acquaintances at Rhytwin, and begged that they would go with him to his hut that evening, that their own eyes might convince them of the truth of what he told them.

'They accordingly went with him to the hut, and after waiting some time, saw, with astonishment, a light settle over the rising ground, and in about ten minutes disappear. They were greatly puzzled to guess at the meaning of this; when at last one of them recollected, that the night before Morgan (that was the name of the murderer) left the country, he happened to pass his hut, and saw a traveller enter.

'This circumstance made him form a suspicion that a murder had been committed; he therefore advised to dig up the rising ground, at the place over which the light had appeared. This was accordingly done, and the body being quickly found, put murder out of all manner of doubt. Those who had found the body deposed all they knew concerning it before a magistrate at Rhytwin. The coroner sat upon it, and brought in his verdict, "Wilful Murder".'

Morgan was apprehended in Bristol, brought back to Wales and found guilty of the labourer's murder. In court, he continued to protest his innocence. Dropping to his knees, he 'prayed to God that his legs might rot off if he was guilty of the murder'. According to the *Terrific Register,* 'between the time of his sentence and execution, they in fact rotted off a little below the knees'. The author continues: 'The hand of God was so visible in this judgement, that the criminal confessed his guilt, and was executed, pursuant to his sentence.'

These thrilling, if unlikely, events took place in 1627. The place named as Rhytwin in the journal possibly refers to Rhydwyn, in Anglesey.

A night-bound traveller marvels at the appearance of a corpse candle in his way.

SORCERY, GHOST OR HOAX?

When I was researching my first ever book on ghosts and folklore many years ago, I came across an extraordinary set of correspondence preserved in the archive of what was then Clwyd County Council. The first letter was written by Robert Roberts, the tenant farmer at Bodeugan, a farm near St Asaph (Llanelwy), in Denbighshire. The letter is dated Christmas 1812, and starts with an apology to Roberts's landlord for the fact that he had failed to supply him with his expected geese.

But the excuse he gives for this lapse is what makes the letter so fascinating. Roberts claims that Bodeugan had become bewitched. He was convinced that 'some malicious person or persons had been with some of the conjurers' whom he believed were then resident in the nearby town of Denbigh.

Here follows an extract of the troubled farmer's account of the dark doings, slightly edited for clarity and with punctuation added (Roberts's letter was entirely devoid of it):

'On the 1st Day of December at night, something began to break the windows by throwing stones and coals and other materials and did so the night following. The day after it began again in the day time, especially in the dairy, to throw down the pots containing churning milk and breaking them to pieces and great many other earthenware and throwing cans and other things at us.

'But that night it was so terrible that the women left the house and went to a neighbour's house. It threw stones, bricks and the like that they had no quiet to milk, by throwing dung upon them. From noon a Thursday till Monday nothing was felt. It began on Monday … threw water and glasses at us that we were so wet as we had been in a river, and shifting many other things …'

All was quiet for ten days. Then, on Christmas Eve, there were further disturbances, 'more dangerous' than before, as Roberts puts it. The servants were kicked and pinched by invisible assailants. Their bedclothes were yanked off the beds and dumped on the floor, sometimes along with the servants. In addition, the unknown force had 'done great deal of damage' during that period. His distracted wife became ill with the stress.

Although Mr Roberts blamed black magic for his troubles, today we would recognise the phenomena experienced at Bodeugan as poltergeist activity. The farmer's landlord asked two friends, a Mr Hughes and a Mr Lloyd, to investigate the strange happenings at Bodeugan. They were impressed by the family's veracity and thought that the disturbances were down to the presence of a spirit rather than witchcraft.

However, while they were visiting the dairy, Mr Hughes and Mr Lloyd spotted one of the servant girls throwing a potato and then a pepper-pot. They challenged her, but she denied throwing either article. The investigators left Bodeugan convinced the servant was the cause of all the mayhem. If the wide range of dramatic incidents outlined by Mr Roberts are to be believed, however, it seems impossible that this girl could possibly have been responsible for them, especially without being detected.

In response to the accusation, Mr Roberts's father-in-law wrote to the landlord in Chester, protesting the girl's innocence. The investigators did concede 'that the Ghost might have made use of her hands to throw things', an insightful as well as diplomatic response. There is evidence to show that people involved in poltergeist cases have contributed to the phenomena without apparently being aware of it. More often, one or two people, particularly young people, can't resist adding to the chaos, either out of devilment, or sometimes – and this may have been the case in the Bodeugan dairy – because the poltergeist has failed to manifest itself and they hate the idea of visitors going away with the idea that the whole thing was a hoax or a delusion.

Unfortunately, the correspondence ends here. If it was a poltergeist at work, however, then it is likely that the phenomena came to an end of their own accord. Thankfully, poltergeists are short-lived spooks, however troublesome they may be when they're around.

THE DEMON DOUBLE

In 1691 an extraordinary book was published by one Richard Baxter. It was called *The Certainty of the World of Spirits*. Like the works of Edmund Jones a century later, Baxter's book was intended to convince the reader that ghosts and other supernatural phenomena existed, and that they were further evidence of the existence of God. *The Certainty of the World of Spirits* is among the earliest books to discuss Welsh folklore and contains within it a strange and disturbing account of a haunting in 'Gowersland' at a house called 'Llanellin'. The house no longer exists, but was in the hamlet now spelled Llanellan, in the northern part of the Gower, near Swansea.

In a series of letters to Baxter, we learn of the remarkable series of events which took place at Llanellin in 1665. The letters were written just a year after they occurred. In those days, the house belonged to a Lieutenant Colonel Bowen, a former Parliamentarian officer during the English Civil War. After the war ended, Bowen went a bit crazy. He declared himself an atheist – a bold thing to do with Oliver Cromwell running the country – and gave himself over to a 'careless and sensual life'. So unruly did Bowen become that he was sent out of England to serve in Ireland. But in Ireland things only got worse. He 'sinned without restraint' and shut himself off from his colleagues and family. One wonders whether he was suffering some form of post-traumatic stress disorder.

Bowen's wife was spared the worst of the indignities because she remained at home in Wales. Nonetheless, the household did not entirely escape the results of his insanity, for one night they were visited by a weird echo of his crazed state of mind. Loud, inexplicable noises were heard throughout the house, including furious bangs on the doors and walls and something described as 'the sound of whirl-wind'. Mrs Bowen was of a very different temperament to her husband. She was still god-fearing and refused to become afraid of empty sounds, however puzzling. She spent some time in prayer and then sensibly retired to her bed.

Then the uniquely horrible aspect of this haunting manifested itself. Shortly after she had got into bed, Mrs Bowen saw 'something like her husband' appear in the room. She knew for certain that Lt Col Bowen was in Ireland, and she realised at once that this was some unearthly facsimile. The apparition spoke to her: it asked whether it could join her in bed! The appalled Mrs Bowen told the intruder it was not her husband and no, it couldn't.

> *'What!' exclaimed the double. 'Not the husband of thy bosom? 'What! 'Not the husband of thy bosom?'*

But it kept its distance. Now there could be no thought of sleep. Mrs Bowen and her servants spent the rest of the night in prayer. On numerous occasions the spectral Lt Col Bowen tried to distract them. The coming of day brought little respite. The spectre did not put in an appearance, but the household were unnerved by seeing on more than one occasion 'the shadow of one walking' cast upon the walls.

The following night the haunting became even more extreme. The 'noise of whirl-wind' was heard again but louder than before, and it was accompanied by chilling howls and screams. When she tried to get into bed, Mrs Bowen saw an impression in the mattress as if a body was lying in it and this was accompanied by the ghastly stench of 'a carcase some-while dead'. Then the invisible corpse began to roll from side to side on the bed. For Mrs Bowen the only response to all this horror was to pray. But as she dropped to her knees, they came into contact with something unseen, something warm and furry like a big dog that rose from the ground, knocking her over. The entire household now resorted to prayer, but this was made difficult for them by eerie cries echoing out of the darkness, and the mumbling of words in a language they could not understand.

Further phenomena followed. The room became suffused with 'a thick smoak [*sic*], smelling like sulphur' and the women were struck and slapped by invisible hands. By dawn the terrified women's faces were black from the smoke and they were 'swollen with bruises'. Later that day mysterious lights appeared in the house and in the fields around it and Lt Col Bowen's voice could be heard, calling as if to his hawks.

The prospect of spending another night in Llanellin was too much to bear and the entire household decamped to safer lodging. Word of the disturbances reached the real Lt Col Bowen and he came home for a visit. He scorned his wife's account of his demon double, however, and refused to accept any of the other bizarre and frightening events which had taken place during his absence. Nothing further took place during his stay.

There is no record of any subsequent phenomena being experienced at Llanellin. It is no surprise to learn that Mrs Bowen soon became estranged from her husband. Lt Col Bowen remained in Ireland and the last heard of him, according to Richard Baxter, is that he had 'immured himself in a small castle, with one boy who said, he oft rose in the night, and talked as if someone were talking with him'. Was he conversing with his own double?

A mansion in the Gower was plagued in the 17th century by a spectral version of the man of the house, even though he was actually hundreds of miles away.

THE BWGANOD

As I have noted before, Welsh ghosts, fairies, and even witches, tended to overlap in people's imaginations in centuries past. Together they might be lumped under the one term, *bwganod,* which might best be translated as 'goblins', or simply 'spooks'. This odd miscellany strikes me as a fitting subject to close this whistlestop tour of Welsh weirdness.

Today we tend to think of ghosts as something akin to video playbacks of people or events that have occurred in the past. Others believe in 'grounded spirits', unfortunate personalities trapped in some kind of limbo, due to unhappiness or sudden death. There is a certain logic to modern ghost-lore. If a person has been murdered, they may continue to haunt the place they were killed. Or perhaps their remorseful murderer might haunt there instead. However, ghosts didn't necessarily follow such straightforward rules in traditional Welsh ghost-lore.

In his *The Folk-Lore of West and Mid Wales,* published in 1911, John Ceredig Davies mentions that 'a poor old woman' had been murdered on a lonely moor near Ystradgynlais and the spot had become haunted as a result. But the moor wasn't haunted by the spirit or apparition of the victim or her killer. Instead it was haunted by 'a ghost which appeared sometimes in the shape of a cat, at other times as a man on horseback'! It was almost as if the tragedy had attracted the *bwgan* but had no direct connection with it.

One of the weirdest examples of a Welsh spook appearing in many different forms comes from Bedwellty in South Wales. In 1760, a group of haymakers saw coming down the hill before them 'an innumerable flock of sheep'; not, you might think, an unusual sight in Wales, but this particular flock suddenly vanished before their astonished eyes. Half an hour before sunset, the vision appeared again, but this time with an extra twist of strangeness: not everyone saw the same thing. Some people saw sheep, as on the previous occasion, but others reported seeing a herd of pigs or a pack of greyhounds. Most bizarrely of all, some people saw a crawling host of naked babies!

This extraordinary account comes from the pen of the Revd Edmund Jones, whom we met previously in regards to changelings. Not only did he believe in fairies, Jones claimed to have seen ghosts, too. His attitude to the supernatural would surprise the modern clergy: he was convinced the appearances of ghosts and fairies were manifestations of God's presence on Earth and not believing in them was the first step towards disbelieving in God. He was a very religious man – but a true eccentric.

The Revd Jones wrote two, now very rare, little books in 1779 and 1780 which showcased encounters with apparitions told to him personally by colleagues and neighbours. Most of these reports are particularly well attested: Jones is able to provide precise details of location and the date of the encounter as well as biographical information about the witness. Yet the stories collected by him are among the strangest ever recorded from the UK.

Thomas Miles Harry, for example, reported an alarming experience near Cwmbran. Returning from Abergavenny one evening, his horse shied, startled by something in the road which he could not see. It bolted for home, Mr Harry clinging on for dear life. In the safety of his own yard, as he was removing the saddle from his trembling horse, he saw what had spooked the animal: the

A RELATION OF

APPARITIONS

OF

SPIRITS,

In the County of Monmouth,

AND THE PRINCIPALITY OF

WALES:

With other notable relations from England ; together with observations about them, and instructions from them : designed to confute and to prevent the infidelity of denying the being and Apparition of Spirits ; which

Tends to Irreligion and Atheism.

By the late Rev. EDMUND JONES, of the *Tranch.*

Nam Sadducæi quidem dicunt non esse resurrectionem, neque angelum, neque spiritum.—Acta xxiii.. 8.

NEWPORT,

MONMOUTHSHIRE:

PRINTED AND SOLD BY E. LEWIS, BOOKSELLER, STATIONER, AND BOOKBINDER; ETHERIDGE AND TIBBINS: SOLD ALSO BY CROSBY AND CO. STATIONER'S-COURT, LONDON; C. FROST, BROAD-STREET, BRISTOL; AND MOST BOOKSELLERS IN TOWN AND COUNTRY.

1813.

The frontispiece to the 1813 edition of Edmund Jones's A Relation of Apparitions of Spirits etc, first published in 1780. This book contains some of the weirdest 'true' ghost stories ever reported from the UK.

apparition of a woman 'so prodigiously tall as to be about half as high as the tall beech trees at the other side of the yard'.

In the same neighbourhood, a Mr Edward Frank had a not dissimilar encounter. Walking home one night he heard footsteps approaching. Then, looming out of the darkness, he saw 'the ghost of a marvellous thin man, whose head was so high above the observer's line of vision that he nearly fell over backwards in his efforts to gaze at it'. He cried out, 'In the name of God, what is there? Turn out of my way or I will strike thee!' The giant ghost vanished at these words and the shaken Mr Frank found a handy cow to lean on while he steadied his nerves!

Many of the spooks recorded by the Revd Jones were sub-human, half-formed shapes lacking detailed features. Two young men, Lewis Thomas and Thomas Andrew, saw on separate occasions in the vicinity of Ebbw Vale a weird, bestial 'resemblance of a man walking on his hands and feet'. Mr Andrew described it as 'creeping on all fours, scraping the ground, and looking aside one way and the other, also making a dreadful noise'.

So many peculiar things were reported to Jones, I can't help wondering whether members of his congregation were making them up just to please him. Many were educated men, however. A schoolmaster named Henry Williams Hugh told Jones he had seen a 'somewhat odd figure' by a stile in Bedwas parish. Something about the man not only alarmed Mr Hugh but also his dog, which ran away. They were right to be nervous – the 'man' suddenly became two men and then the pair of them disappeared in 'a pillar of fire'. When Mr Hugh got home, he found his dog had been so scared that it had hidden its head in a pot and become stuck.

Perhaps the strangest of all these strange apparitions was the one described to Jones by a dairymaid at a farm near Pontypool. It was roughly the shape of a man but 'very big in the middle and narrow at both ends', and when the girl's dog approached it, it shot out a long, black tongue, scaring it away. With a heavy, earth-shaking tread, the monster then marched off in the direction of a spring named, intriguingly enough, Ffynnon yr Yspryd ('Well of the Spirit'), where it vanished.

I can only say I am delighted such weird denizens of the Welsh countryside are now a thing of the past. I certainly wouldn't stray far from my door after dark if I thought any of them were still lurking about!

OTHER TITLES FROM BRADWELL BOOKS

LEGENDS & FOLKLORE

Nottinghamshire
Scotland
Wiltshire

GHOST STORIES

Cambridgeshire
Cheshire
Cotswolds
Cumbrian
Dorset
Essex
Hampshire & the Isle of Wight
Kent
Lancashire
London
Norfolk
North Wales
Oxfordshire
Scottish
Somerset
South Wales
Surrey
Sussex
Yorkshire

OTHER TITLES

Black Country & Birmingham (Brendan Hawthorne)

Cornish (A Corn)

Derbyshire (Jill Armitage)

Leicestershire (David Bell)

London Underground (Jill Armitage)

Staffordshire (David Bell)

Welsh Celebrity Ghost Stories (South Wales Paranormal Research)

For more information visit
www.bradwellbooks.com